EUROPEAN COUNTRIES TODAY
BELGIUM

EUROPEAN COUNTRIES TODAY
TITLES IN THE SERIES

Austria	**Italy**
Belgium	**Netherlands**
Czech Republic	**Poland**
Denmark	**Portugal**
France	**Spain**
Germany	**Sweden**
Greece	**United Kingdom**
Ireland	**European Union Facts & Figures**

EUROPEAN COUNTRIES TODAY
BELGIUM

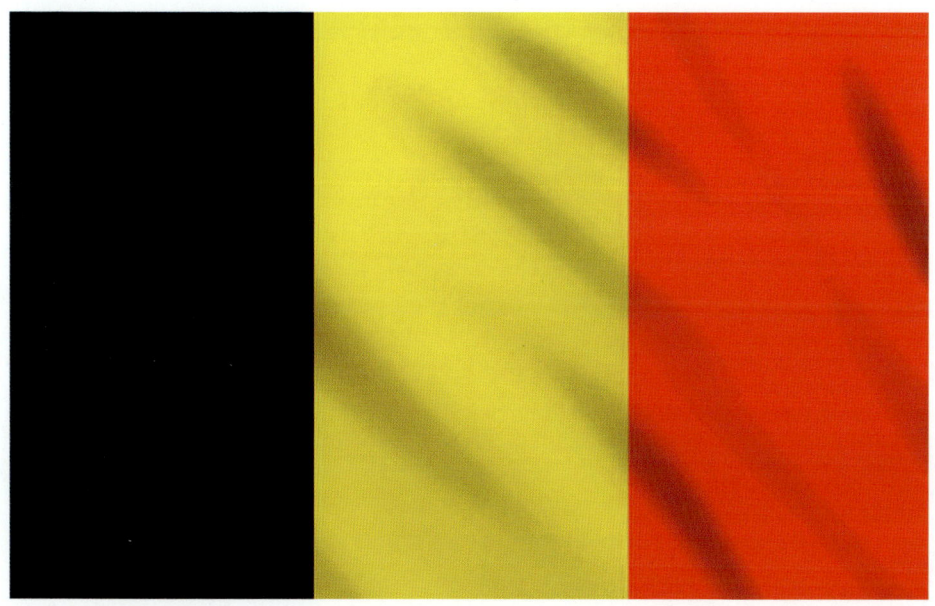

Dominic J. Ainsley

MASON CREST

Mason Crest
450 Parkway Drive, Suite D
Broomall, Pennsylvania PA 19008
(866) MCP-BOOK (toll free)

Copyright © 2019 by Mason Crest, an imprint of National Highlights, Inc. All rights reserved. No part of this publication may be reproduced or transmitted in any form or by any means, electronic or mechanical, including photocopying, recording, taping, or any information storage and retrieval system, without permission in writing from the publisher.

First printing
9 8 7 6 5 4 3 2 1

ISBN: 978-1-4222-3979-7
Series ISBN: 978-4222-3977-3
ebook ISBN: 978-1-4222-7794-2

Printed in the United States of America

Library of Congress Cataloging-in-Publication Data

Names: Ainsley, Dominic J., author.
Title: Belgium / Dominic J. Ainsley.
Description: Broomall, Pennsylvania : Mason Crest, 2019. | Includes index.
Identifiers: LCCN 2018007570 (print) | LCCN 2018018310 (ebook) | ISBN 9781422277942 (eBook) | ISBN 9781422239797 (hardback) | ISBN 9781422239773 (series)
Subjects: LCSH: Belgium--Juvenile literature.
Classification: LCC DH418 (ebook) | LCC DH418 .A36 2019 (print) | DDC 949.3--dc23
LC record available at https://lccn.loc.gov/2018007570

Cover images
Main: *Horst Castle, near Aarschot.*
Left: *Belgian chocolates.*
Center: *Procession of the Holy Blood, Bruges.*
Right: *European Parliament Building, Brussels.*

QR CODES AND LINKS TO THIRD-PARTY CONTENT

You may gain access to certain third-party content ("Third- Party Sites") by scanning and using the QR Codes that appear in this publication (the "QR Codes"). We do not operate or control in any respect any information, products, or services on such Third-Party Sites linked to by us via the QR Codes included in this publication, and we assume no responsibility for any materials you may access using the QR Codes. Your use of the QR Codes may be subject to terms, limitations, or restrictions set forth in the applicable terms of use or otherwise established by the owners of the Third-Party Sites. Our linking to such Third-Party Sites via the QR Codes does not imply an endorsement or sponsorship of such Third-Party Sites or the information, products, or services offered on or through the Third-Party Sites, nor does it imply an endorsement or sponsorship of this publication by the owners of such Third-Party Sites.

CONTENTS

Belgium at a Glance	6
Chapter 1: Belgium's Geography & Landscape	11
Chapter 2: The Government & History of Belgium	25
Chapter 3: The Belgian Economy	45
Chapter 4: Citizens of Belgium: People, Customs & Culture	57
Chapter 5: The Famous Cities of Belgium	71
Chapter 6: A Bright Future for Belgium	87
Chronology	90
Further Reading & Internet Resources	91
Index	92
Picture Credits & Author	96

KEY ICONS TO LOOK FOR:

Words to Understand: These words with their easy-to-understand definitions will increase the reader's understanding of the text while building vocabulary skills.

Sidebars: This boxed material within the main text allows readers to build knowledge, gain insights, explore possibilities, and broaden their perspectives by weaving together additional information to provide realistic and holistic perspectives.

Educational Videos: Readers can view videos by scanning our QR codes, providing them with additional content to supplement the text. Examples include news coverage, moments in history, speeches, iconic sports moments, and much more!

Text-Dependent Questions: These questions send the reader back to the text for more careful attention to the evidence presented there.

Research Projects: Readers are pointed toward areas of further inquiry connected to each chapter. Suggestions are provided for projects that encourage deeper research and analysis.

BELGIUM AT A GLANCE

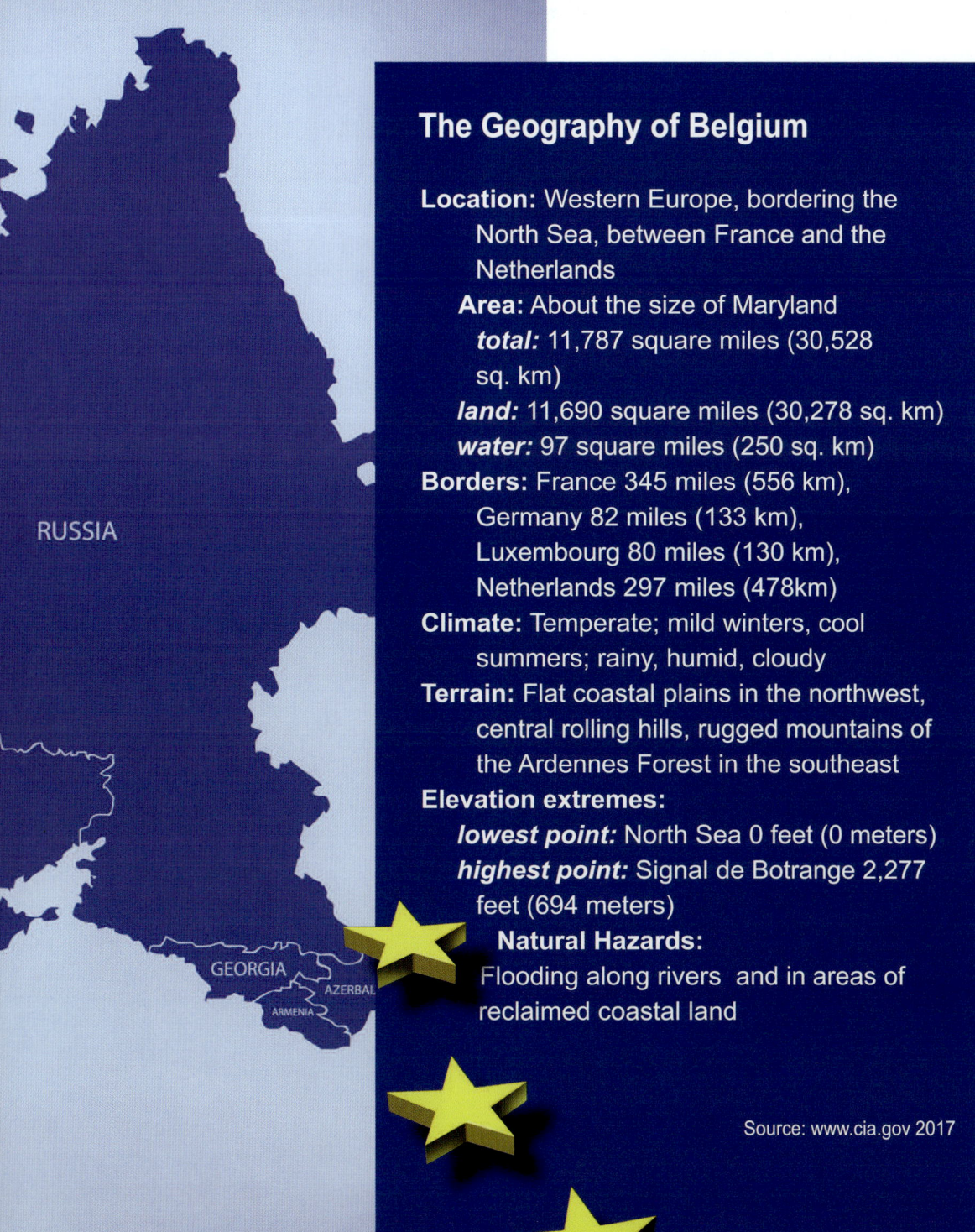

The Geography of Belgium

Location: Western Europe, bordering the North Sea, between France and the Netherlands

Area: About the size of Maryland
  total: 11,787 square miles (30,528 sq. km)
  land: 11,690 square miles (30,278 sq. km)
  water: 97 square miles (250 sq. km)

Borders: France 345 miles (556 km), Germany 82 miles (133 km), Luxembourg 80 miles (130 km), Netherlands 297 miles (478km)

Climate: Temperate; mild winters, cool summers; rainy, humid, cloudy

Terrain: Flat coastal plains in the northwest, central rolling hills, rugged mountains of the Ardennes Forest in the southeast

Elevation extremes:
  lowest point: North Sea 0 feet (0 meters)
  highest point: Signal de Botrange 2,277 feet (694 meters)

Natural Hazards: Flooding along rivers and in areas of reclaimed coastal land

Source: www.cia.gov 2017

BELGIUM AT A GLANCE

Flag of Belgium

Belgium has quite varied terrain with the Ardennes (lying to the southeast of the country) comprising moorland, woodland, and peat bogs, and the lowland plains making up the rest. The Kingdom of Belgium is strategically placed within Europe and is referred to as one of the "Low Countries." Its population consists of Dutch Flemish-speaking and French Walloon-speaking peoples, with a small German minority. Each province has its own flag, while that of Belgium derives from the arms of the provinces of Brabant, Flanders, and Hainault. Although the flag is based on the French tricolor, it is interesting to note that it is almost square in shape.

BELOW: Belgium's North Sea coast is known for its sand dunes. This beach is near De Haan, which is a popular tourist resort.

8

EUROPEAN COUNTRIES TODAY: BELGIUM

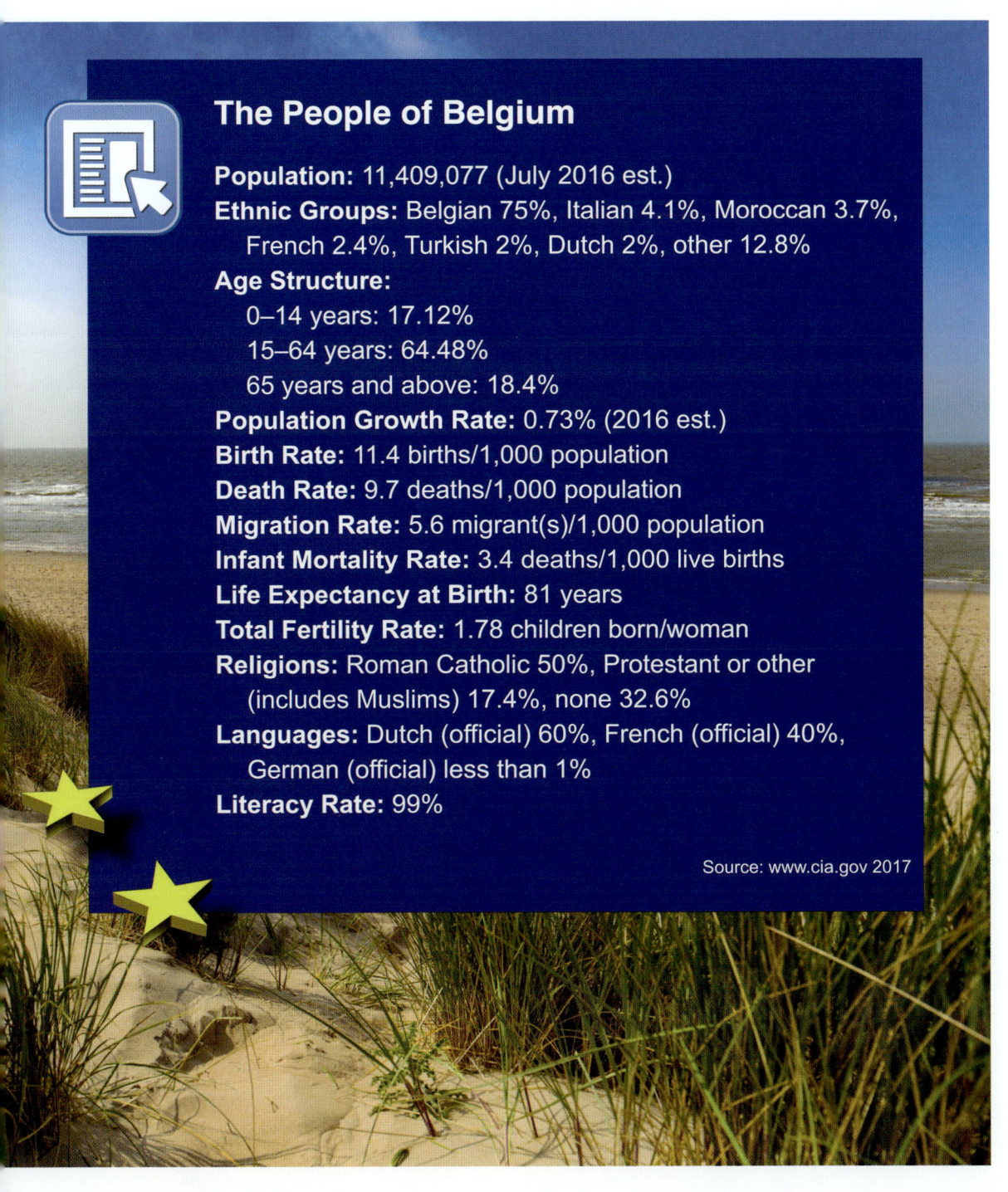

The People of Belgium

Population: 11,409,077 (July 2016 est.)
Ethnic Groups: Belgian 75%, Italian 4.1%, Moroccan 3.7%, French 2.4%, Turkish 2%, Dutch 2%, other 12.8%
Age Structure:
  0–14 years: 17.12%
  15–64 years: 64.48%
  65 years and above: 18.4%
Population Growth Rate: 0.73% (2016 est.)
Birth Rate: 11.4 births/1,000 population
Death Rate: 9.7 deaths/1,000 population
Migration Rate: 5.6 migrant(s)/1,000 population
Infant Mortality Rate: 3.4 deaths/1,000 live births
Life Expectancy at Birth: 81 years
Total Fertility Rate: 1.78 children born/woman
Religions: Roman Catholic 50%, Protestant or other (includes Muslims) 17.4%, none 32.6%
Languages: Dutch (official) 60%, French (official) 40%, German (official) less than 1%
Literacy Rate: 99%

Source: www.cia.gov 2017

Words to Understand

Flanders: The Dutch-speaking northern region of Belgium that includes West and East Flanders.

grottoes: Caves or recesses, formed over thousands of years. Grottoes can also be man-made.

topographical: Relating to the surface features of an area or locality.

ABOVE: The town of Bouillon, Luxembourg on the Semois River. The medieval castle in the background is situated on a rocky spur above the town.

Chapter One
BELGIUM'S GEOGRAPHY & LANDSCAPE

If a country could be compared to a food, Belgium would be best described as a walnut. A tiny nation, no bigger than the state of Maryland, the Kingdom of Belgium consists of two distinct halves.

The Dutch-speaking region of **Flanders** lies in the north, and Wallonia, the French-speaking region, is in the south. Brussels, the capital city, which lies right in the center of the country, joins the two regions linguistically and geographically.

Europe's Great Meeting Place

Belgium has always been linked to both commercial and cultural exchange. Much of the country's character is due to its role as the great meeting place of Western Europe. Located in northwestern Europe, traces of the Austrians, Spanish, French, and Dutch can still be seen in its architecture and in the lifestyle of its people.

Belgium mirrors many characteristics of its neighbors as well: the lowlands of the Netherlands in the north and northeast, the daunting Alps of Germany in the east, the rolling hills of Luxembourg in the southeast, and the fertile plain and deep valleys of France in the southwest and west. Its coastline stretches forty-one miles (66 kilometers) along the North Sea in the northwest. England lies just over the English Channel. No wonder Brussels is called the "Capital of Europe!"

Flanders

Flanders is Belgium's Dutch-speaking northern region. Combined with the Dutch lowlands, Flanders forms a plain on the southern coast of the North Sea.

BELGIUM'S GEOGRAPHY & LANDSCAPE

Educational Video

This 10 minute video provides a brief insight into Belgium's geography. Scan the QR code with your phone to watch!

Flanders is divided into three **topographical** zones. The Polder Zone is the coastal plain, never reaching more than nine miles (14 kilometers) wide at any point. Altitudes in the region range from zero to 164 feet (50 meters).

Reaching from the Polder Zone to the river Scheldt are the Flemish Plains. The landscape is mostly flat, with the highest altitude being sixty-five feet (20 meters). A line of hills occasionally breaks through the region's flatlands.

ABOVE: *The river Scheldt near the Flemish village of Vlassenbroek, Flanders.*

EUROPEAN COUNTRIES TODAY: BELGIUM

The Kempen Plains are Belgium's most sparsely populated region. The sandy plain, broken by bogs, moors, and marshes, extends into the Netherlands. The area is not completely flat; it is a region of rolling land.

Almost 58 percent of the country's total population is found in Flanders. Its location on the continent has made it the "distribution platform" of Europe. It is a transportation and industrial center for Belgium and Europe.

Many of the towns and cities of Flanders have been historically preserved, representing the various cultures found in the region. At the same time, many towns have all the modern technological conveniences that individuals and businesses need in the twenty-first century.

ABOVE: *The Hoeke Windmill was built in 1840. It is a protected monument. In recent years it has been restored and is used to grind grain again.*

BELGIUM'S GEOGRAPHY & LANDSCAPE

Red Flanders Poppy

The common poppy, also known as the Flanders poppy, is the national flower of Belgium. It was a common sight among the trenches and battlefields during World War I, and has become synonymous with the great loss of life during that war. Today, the poppy is associated with World Wars I and II.

To see such beautiful flowers growing across fields where thousands of men died leaves an impression on the minds of all those who witness them.

Wallonia

In the south lies the French-speaking region of Wallonia. Here, the flatlands are replaced by the rolling hills of the Ardennes and the fertile valley beyond.

The Ardennes in the southeast are forested and hilly, with steep river valleys. The valleys of the river Meuse are especially steep. Here, one finds the highest point in Belgium, the Signal de Botrange, at an elevation of 2,277 feet (694 meters). Sparsely populated, with only 125 inhabitants per square mile, the region is predominantly rural. Its loamy, chalky soil is suitable for agriculture.

South of the Ardennes, the hills give way to wide fertile valleys where most of Belgium's crops are grown. Sugar beet, potatoes, wheat, barley, apples, tomatoes, oats, corn (maize), chicory (endive), and flax are all cultivated here.

A characteristic feature of the region is its many **grottoes**. The caves have been formed over thousands of years as water containing carbonic acid has carved a path through the chalky rock.

EUROPEAN COUNTRIES TODAY: BELGIUM

ABOVE: *The Caves of Han are a network of underground caves in Han-sur-Lesse, close to Rochefort, in the Belgian province of Namur.*

BELGIUM'S GEOGRAPHY & LANDSCAPE

Although overlooked by industry, the region provides Belgium with its building materials. There are considerable supplies of chalk and limestone, as well as building stone, including granite, sandstone, and marble.

Although Wallonia lags behind Flanders in economic might, its cities are centers of excellence in their own right. Liège is the center of Belgium's steel industry, while Namur is the transportation hub of the Ardennes region. Tournai, along the French border, is Belgium's most important art center as well as one of the oldest cities.

ABOVE: *Warchenne "quartzite" quarry near the town of Waimes in Liège province.*

EUROPEAN COUNTRIES TODAY: BELGIUM

ABOVE: The Buda Bridge (Budabrug) is an industrial lifting bridge on the ship canal in Brussels. It was opened in 1955 by Prince Albert.

Brussels: The Meeting Point

Brussels, Belgium's capital city, serves as the meeting point between the country's deep linguistic and geographic divides. Situated right in the middle of the country, the city unites many aspects of Belgium.

A French-speaking city in a Flemish-speaking region, Brussels brings within its fold the waterways of Flanders (the Senne, a tributary of the Scheldt, flows through the city) and the hills of Wallonia (the city is situated upon several hills).

17

BELGIUM'S GEOGRAPHY & LANDSCAPE

During the past century, the river has been completely built over within the center of the city. Corresponding to its hill character, Brussels falls naturally into two parts: the Upper and Lower Cities, the latter of which includes the old part of the town.

Today, Brussels is one of the world's great cosmopolitan cities, home to both the European Union (EU) and the North Atlantic Treaty Organization (NATO), plus over fifty intergovernmental agencies, as well as countless trade associations and many international companies. Most of the city's residents, many of whom are foreigners, either work in one of these agencies or are engaged in industrial activity and labor.

ABOVE: *Dinant is a Walloon city and municipality located on the river Meuse in the Belgian province of Namur. It is positioned in the upper Meuse valley at a point where the river cuts deeply into the western Condroz plateau.*

EUROPEAN COUNTRIES TODAY: BELGIUM

ABOVE: *Antwerp is on the North Sea coast. The old town is known for its cosmopolitan mix of restaurants.*

The Provinces

Although Belgium is geographically divided into three regions, the country has ten administrative provinces. The ten provinces are: West Flanders, bordering the North Sea; East Flanders, Antwerp, and Limburg to the north; Walloon Brabant, Flemish Brabant, and the capital Brussels, in the center; Liège to the east; Hainaut to the southwest; Namur to the south; and Luxembourg (not to be confused with Belgium's neighbor the Grand Duchy of Luxembourg) to the southeast.

Rivers of Prosperity

Throughout Belgium's history, its rivers have been the bearers of prosperity. The two main rivers are the Scheldt, which flows through most of Flanders, and the Meuse, which enriches parts of Wallonia. These rivers bring wealth to the towns of Tournai, Ghent, Antwerp, Liège, and Namur.

BELGIUM'S GEOGRAPHY & LANDSCAPE

A Temperate Climate

Relatively mild summers, cool winters, and wet westerly and southwesterly winds characterize Belgium's temperate climate. A sudden shower can erupt out of a perfectly sunny day. This has made umbrellas and raincoats a permanent fixture in all Belgian homes.

The average winter temperature varies from 37°F (2.8°C) in the coastal areas to 32°F (0°C) in the center, and a freezing 30°F (-1°C) in the Ardennes. The corresponding summer temperatures in those areas are 61°F (16°C) on the coast, 66°F (18.9°C) in the center, and 57°F (13.9°C) in the Ardennes. The country's annual average rainfall is approximately thirty to forty inches (762 to 1,016 millimeters).

ABOVE: A wooden walkway through the frozen landscape of the Hautes Fagnes (High Fens). The area is an important nature reserve in the east of Belgium.

EUROPEAN COUNTRIES TODAY: BELGIUM

Eurasian Red Squirrel

This attractive squirrel inhabits the woodland areas of Belgium and is particularly widespread in the Ardennes. Red squirrels feed on shoots, pine cones, and other seeds, storing excess items in hollow trees or in holes in the ground. Stripped pine cones, scattered about the woodland floor, can point to the fact that the species has been active. The red squirrel's nest is known as a dray which is a relatively small, compact structure. Red squirrels produce one or two litters of about three young each year. The red squirrel has sharp claws, and consequently, is very good at climbing. Its curved claws enable it to climb and descend both large and small tress. With strong hind legs, it excels at leaping between gaps in the trees. The red squirrel also has the ability to swim. Red squirrels that survive their first winter have a life expectancy of three years.

Plants & Animals

Although Belgium is famous for its brussels sprouts (grown in abundance all over Belgium), the country is not a major agricultural producer. The country has no permanent crops, and less than 30 percent of its land is arable. Agricultural produce includes sugar beet, fresh vegetables, fruits, grain, tobacco, beef, veal, pork, and milk.

Broad-leaved deciduous trees such as the oak, beech, and elm cover most of Belgium's forestland. The country's biggest nature reserve, Hautes Fagnes, lies at the northeasten edge of the Ardennes, along the border with Germany. Once

21

BELGIUM'S GEOGRAPHY & LANDSCAPE

covered with peat bogs, the area has now been forested with spruce. Coniferous forests are found at higher elevations, and mixed coniferous and deciduous trees, especially beech and oak, grow in the foothills.

Since Belgium is very urbanized, most if its wild animals are found in the Ardennes. Wild boars, wildcats, deer, red squirrels, and pheasant are among the more common animals of the region. A number of birds can be found in Belgium's lowlands, including sandpipers, woodcocks, snipes, and lapwings. The area north of the Ardennes is home to a considerable population of muskrats and hamsters.

ABOVE: The famous panoramic view of the Giant's Tomb lying inside the bend of the river Semois. It is located near the city of Bouillon, Wallonia in the Ardennes.

EUROPEAN COUNTRIES TODAY: BELGIUM

ABOVE: *The Belgian Blue is a breed native to Belgium. Usually it is bred for its beef but can be used for dairy production too.*

Text-Dependent Questions

1. How many different languages are spoken in Belgium?

2. Where is Wallonia?

3. What are Belgium's most important rivers?

Research Project

The Ardennes is an unspoiled region of Belgium. Describe its wildlife, geography, and tourist attractions. Use a map to locate the region and then describe how you would arrange a trip there.

23

Words to Understand

civil war: A war between opposing groups from the same country.

constitutional monarchy: A system in which a country is ruled by a king and/or queen whose power is limited by a constitution.

Crusades: Military expeditions undertaken by Christian powers in medieval times to win the Holy Land from the Muslims.

BELOW: The twelfth-century Beersel Castle is located in the town of Beersel in Flemish Brabant, south of Brussels.

Chapter Two
THE GOVERNMENT & HISTORY OF BELGIUM

Belgium has played an important part in Europe's history. Since it was strategically located between Europe and England, a series of empires wrestled for control of its trade routes and industries.

The Kingdom of Belgium as we know it today came into existence in 1830. Until then, it was a part of the United Kingdom of the Netherlands. Belgium won its independence from the Dutch as a result of an uprising of the Belgian people. A **constitutional monarchy** was established in 1831, and Leopold of Saxe-Coburg was appointed king of Belgium.

Celtic Roots

Belgium's recorded history can be traced back about two thousand years. Belgium was then part of a much larger region that the Romans called Gaul. Gaul comprised the entire west European region. Today, this area is made up of France, Belgium, western Switzerland, and parts of the Netherlands.

Belgium derives its name from a Celtic tribe, the Belgae, whom Julius Caesar

ABOVE: *Charlemagne by Albrecht Dürer.*

THE GOVERNMENT & HISTORY OF BELGIUM

Educational Video

Belgium Explained: Language and political structure.

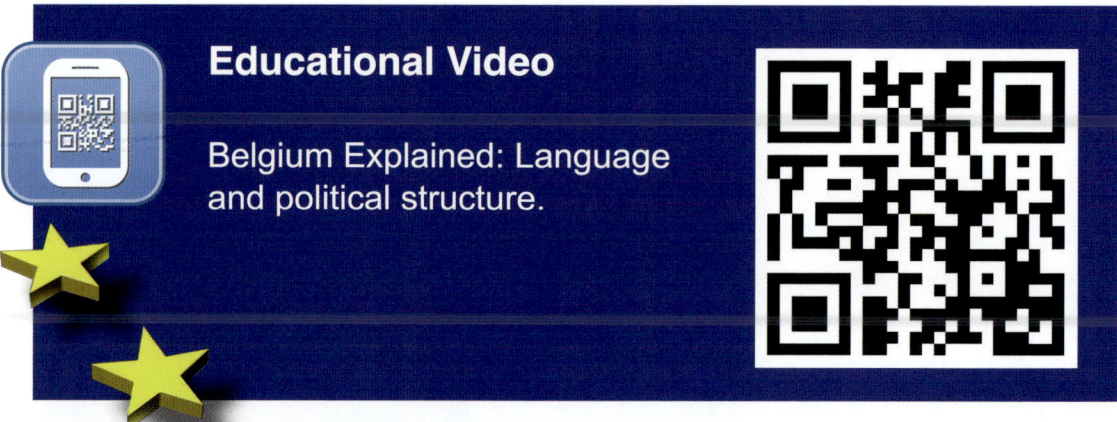

ABOVE: La Roche-en-Ardenne in the Ardennes. The ruins of the town's medieval castle date back to the eleventh century. It is situated on a rocky outcrop above the town.

EUROPEAN COUNTRIES TODAY: BELGIUM

described as the most courageous tribe of Gaul. However, the Belgae were forced to yield to Roman legions during the first century BCE. For the next three hundred years, the region that is now Belgium flourished as a province of Rome.

After the collapse of the Roman Empire in 406 CE, the Franks invaded the region. They were a loose confederation of Germanic tribes who had been pushed out of Germany by Attila the Hun. Under the Franks, Christianity spread, and churches and monasteries were built across the entire region.

Charlemagne: Holy Roman Emperor

Under the rule of Emperor Charlemagne, the Frankish Empire extended from the Elbe to the Atlantic, and from the North Sea to the Mediterranean. As a result, in 800 CE, the pope himself crowned Charlemagne as the first Holy Roman Emperor. After his death, the empire was divided between his sons.

Dating Systems and Their Meaning

You might be accustomed to seeing dates expressed with the abbreviations BC or AD, as in the year 1000 BC or the year AD 1900. For centuries, this dating system has been the most common in the Western world. However, since BC and AD are based on Christianity (BC stands for Before Christ and AD stands for anno Domini, Latin for "in the year of our Lord"), many people now prefer to use abbreviations that people from all religions can be comfortable using. The abbreviations BCE (meaning Before Common Era) and CE (meaning Common Era), mark time in the same way (for example, 1000 BC is the same year as 1000 BCE, and AD 1900 is the same year as 1900 CE), but BCE and CE do not have the same religious overtones as BC and AD.

Gravensteen, Ghent

The Gravensteen was the medieval stronghold of the counts of Flanders, and though now near the center of Ghent, it would have been outside the town in the ninth century when it was first built. The site offered no natural topographical advantages, and the castle was protected by a wide moat, which nonetheless, failed to prevent two successful sieges in the fourteenth century. By 1539, however, the counts had moved out and the castle had passed into the hands of the dukes of Burgundy. Thereafter, the history of the Gravensteen was less important and less violent. Various parts were converted into government offices and, for a time in the nineteenth century, even a factory.

The castle has an unusual appearance, chiefly due to the hanging turrets along the curtain wall, allowing covering fire for the walls, which may have derived from experience of the **Crusades**. There are other indications of familiarity with Byzantine practice and the chapel has an unusual window in the form of a cross. Another striking feature is the gatehouse, defended by machicolated towers, which is large enough to suggest a kind of subsidiary castle in itself. The keep, with large halls on two floors, is massive, and still dominates the city. The castle contains the usual horrors: a torture

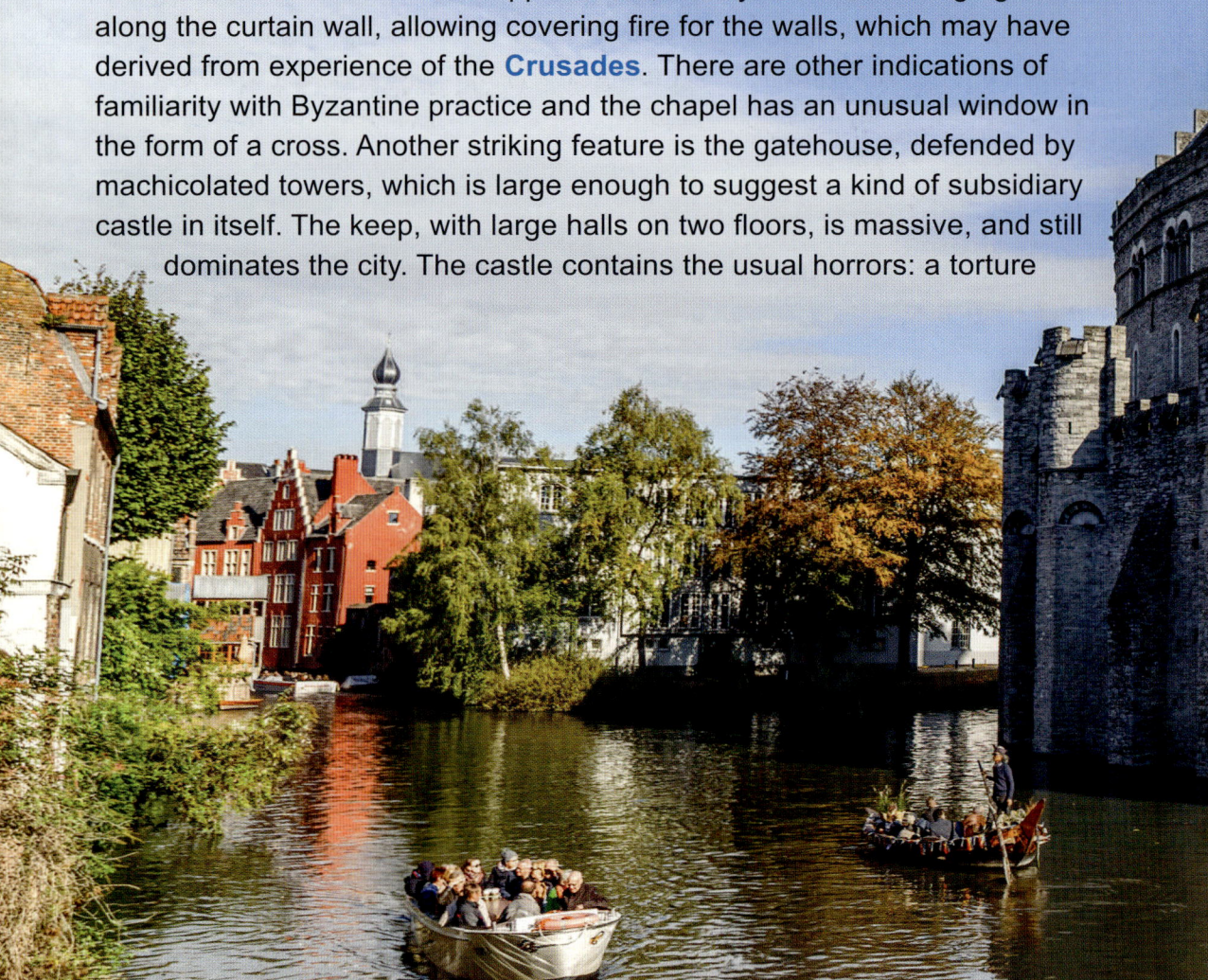

chamber and an *oubliette*, which was entered only by a trapdoor in the ceiling (and rarely left again).

There are some remains of the original building in the base of the keep; otherwise, the Gravensteen today looks like an unusually well-preserved thirteenth-century castle, though this is chiefly due to careful restoration in the late nineteenth century.

THE GOVERNMENT & HISTORY OF BELGIUM

The Rise of Flanders

The fall of the Frankish Empire created a power vacuum. Baldwin the Iron Arm from Flanders profited from the weakness of the French throne to become a strong leader. From the twelfth century onward, the blossoming of trade between the Continent (continental Europe) and England resulted in the rapid growth of the cities in Flanders.

Bruges became the trading center for goods from Italy, France, Germany, and England. The growing textile industry was also a vital factor in the increasing wealth and prestige of the cities, although this industry relied on a steady supply of wool from England.

The Hundred Years' War between France and England began in 1337. Flanders sided with the French against England, causing England to boycott and cease sending wool there. Trade in Flanders came to a complete halt. To get the economy back on its feet, merchants and craftsmen rebelled against their rulers to reestablish trade with England. Trade blossomed once again, bringing back old conflicts of interests between merchants and craftsmen. As tensions came to a boil, a full-fledged civil war robbed Flanders of all power it had gained.

ABOVE: *Philip, Duke of Burgundy by Rogier van der Weyden.*

ABOVE: *Marie of Burgundy accredited to Michael Pacher.*

EUROPEAN COUNTRIES TODAY: BELGIUM

ABOVE: *Maximilian I, Holy Roman Emperor by Albrecht Dürer.*

THE GOVERNMENT & HISTORY OF BELGIUM

The Golden Age of the Burgundians
In the early fifteenth century, Philip, the duke of Burgundy, married the daughter and heiress of the count of Flanders. After the count's death, Belgian Flanders, Artois, and other territories were incorporated into the Burgundian duchy. The Burgundian household now controlled an area comprising today's Netherlands and Belgium.

The Burgundian era was a tense period of history. But amid the ravages of war, the art world of Flanders flourished.

Belgium Under Spanish Rule
In 1477, Marie of Burgundy married Austrian ruler Maximilian, a member of the Habsburg family. Maximilian's grandson inherited the Spanish crown (and eventually the crown of Holy Roman Emperor), bringing Belgium under Spanish influence. This ignited a long battle against Catholic Spanish rule.

During the sixteenth century, Dutch-speaking parts of the Netherlands became Protestant, while the southern, Flemish parts remained Roman Catholic. The Catholic king of Spain, Philip II, strictly suppressed Protestantism during the mid-sixteenth century, especially in Flanders. Thousands were imprisoned or executed before full-scale war erupted in 1568. The Revolt of the Netherlands lasted eighty years, and in the end, Protestant Holland and its allied provinces booted out the Spaniards. The dominantly Catholic areas of Belgium and Luxembourg stayed under Spanish rule.

Austria Takes Over
The death of Charles II, the last of the Spanish Habsburgs, effectively ended the Spanish rule of Belgium. In the ensuing power struggle, Belgium passed into Austria's hands.

Belgium experienced enormous economic prosperity under the Austrian queen Maria Theresa. Trade and industry grew. Roads were built, linking important cities such as Brussels and Vienna. Arts and crafts also reached their zenith. Tournai was a manufacturing center for porcelain. The fashion for lace reached its peak, and architecture flourished.

EUROPEAN COUNTRIES TODAY: BELGIUM

ABOVE: *Maria Theresa by Martin van Meytens.*

THE GOVERNMENT & HISTORY OF BELGIUM

Tossed Between Nations

Toward the latter part of the eighteenth century, revolts broke out across Belgium, leading to the formation of the United States of Belgium, a loose conglomeration of sovereign states. In 1794, the troops of the new Austrian emperor, Leopold II, forcibly brought Belgium back into the Austrian fold.

The following year, during the Austrian and Prussian war against Revolutionary France, Napoleonic France beat the Austrian army. France occupied both Belgium and the Netherlands, which were combined and renamed the Batavian Republic. Belgium remained under French dominion for the next twenty years.

With the defeat of Napoleon's army at the Battle of Waterloo, fought just a few miles south of Brussels, Belgium was separated from France. In 1815, the Congress of Vienna made Belgium part of the Netherlands. The new United Kingdom of the Netherlands was ruled by the Dutch House of Orange.

In 1830, Belgium won its independence from the Dutch as a result of an uprising of the Belgian people. The French-speaking minority controlled the factories and other economic resources. They did not want to live under a Dutch-speaking administration, and they mounted a revolution. The fact that Belgium was mostly Catholic and the Netherlands predominantly Protestant also played a role.

A constitutional monarchy was established in 1831. King Leopold I from the House of Saxe-Coburg in Germany was invited to be monarch. To celebrate Belgium's hard-won freedom, July 21 was proclaimed a day of national rejoicing.

ABOVE: *King Leopold I by George Dawe.*

Belgium and Colonialism

In 1865, Leopold II became king. His first act as king was to satisfy his colonial ambitions. Through a policy of murder, deception, and colonialism, Leopold gained control of the entire Congo basin in Africa. He made the land his private property and called it the Congo Free State. Here, the local population was brutalized in exchange for rubber. In 1908, under international pressure, Leopold II was forced to give his property to the Belgian state as a colony. From then onward, it became the Belgian Congo until it gained its independence from Belgium in 1960.

World War I

Belgium was one of the bloodiest battlegrounds of World War I. The area around Ypres witnessed some of the worst fighting of the entire war, with huge loss of life on both sides. For the first time in war, poison gas was used—first chlorine gas in 1915 and then mustard gas in 1917.

Although Germany defeated Belgium, after the war, Belgium was able to regain its territories, as well as additional German-speaking regions in Eupen-Malmedy. It was also given the former German colonies of Rwanda and Burundi in Africa.

World War II

To counter Germany's continued aggression after World War I, Belgium's King Albert I declared his nation a neutral country in 1936. His declaration did little good. On May 10, 1940, German troops invaded Belgium. As the Nazi forces scoured Belgium for

ABOVE: *Leopold II.*

THE GOVERNMENT & HISTORY OF BELGIUM

Battle of Passchendaele
July 31 to November 6, 1917

The World War I Battle of Passchendaele is officially known as the Third Battle of Ypres. It is infamous for its very high level of casualties. The infantry attack began on July 31, 1917. The constant shelling smashed the drainage system, causing heavy flooding. The quagmire of thick mud clogged up the rifles and immobilized the tanks. The mud was so deep that men and horses were drowned. Following the flooding, stalemate reigned for another month. Eventually, in the following weeks, the village of Passchendaele was captured by the British and Canadians. The offensive was called off on November 6, with Field Marshal Sir Douglas Haig claiming success.

Jews, the Belgian spirit rose to the occasion. Many Belgians showed great courage in their commitment to aid the persecuted and became active in the Resistance.

But by the time the Allied forces freed the last Belgian city in 1945, Belgium was in ruins. The task of rebuilding the nation now lay ahead.

Building Partnerships

The German invasions during the two world wars made Belgium one of the foremost advocates of collective security within the framework of European integration and the Atlantic partnership.

In 1948, the customs and economic union BENELUX (Belgium, the Netherlands, and Luxembourg) was formed. These countries, along with France, West Germany, and Italy, formed the European Coal and Steel Community "to substitute for age-old rivalries the merging of essential interest."

EUROPEAN COUNTRIES TODAY: BELGIUM

ABOVE: *The Menin Gate, Ypres, is a World War I memorial inscribed with 54,389 names of the missing from the battle area of Ypres Salient. It was unveiled on July 24, 1927.*

THE GOVERNMENT & HISTORY OF BELGIUM

In 1957, the same countries signed the Treaty of Rome, which established the European Economic Community (EEC), which has now become the European Union or the EU.

Rebuilding Belgium

Compared to its neighboring countries, Belgium's economic recovery after the world wars was rapid. The harbor of Antwerp had been spared major damage during the conflict, and the country's energy reserves were adequate to supply all the necessary power.

In May 1945, exiled King Leopold III returned to Belgium to hostile citizens. After fierce protests between groups that supported him and those who wanted the monarchy abolished, Leopold abdicated in favor of his son Baudouin I. Economic prosperity followed the change in leadership.

Belgium Today

Since 1970, three communities and three regions have existed within Belgium: the Flemish, the French, and the German-speaking communities; and the Flemish, the Walloon, and the Brussels regions.

In 1980, measures were taken to expand the authority of the regions, which were granted their own rights and institutions. Today, although Belgium is a constitutional monarchy with a parliamentary form of government, the country has a complex system of municipalities, provinces, and regions as well as a centralized state.

The central state has authority in national defense, foreign affairs, social issues, agriculture, justice, and financial and monetary issues. Policymaking areas such as the economy, education, transport, and the environment have all been passed on to the regions.

In 1993, King Baudouin's brother, Albert II, took over the throne. After his ascension, Belgium reformed the bicameral parliamentary system and provided for the direct election of the members of community and regional legislative councils. In 2013, Albert II abdicated for health reasons. His son Philippe ascended the throne on July 21, 2013.

EUROPEAN COUNTRIES TODAY: BELGIUM

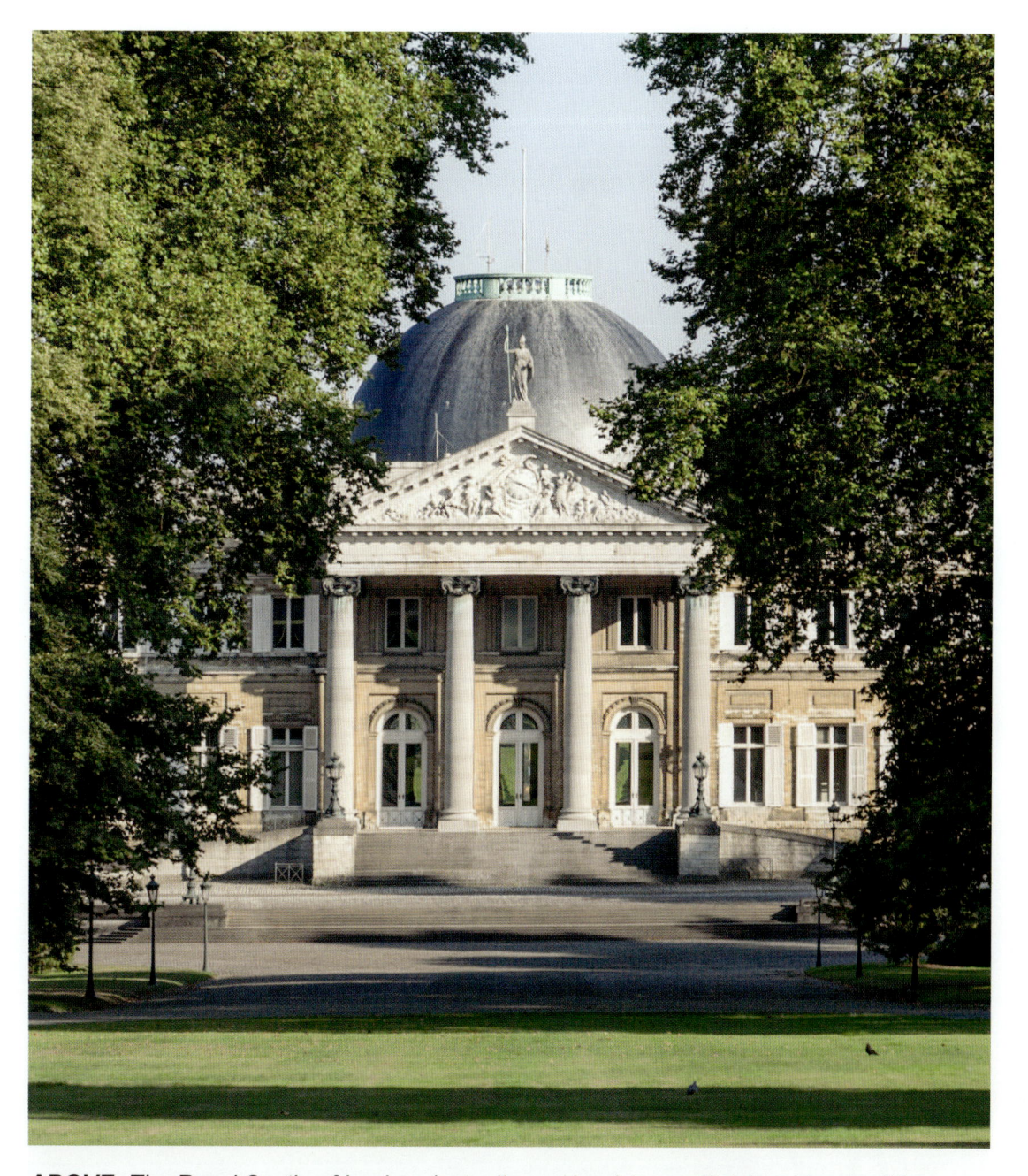

ABOVE: The Royal Castle of Laeken (actually a palace) is an official residence of the Belgian royal family.

THE GOVERNMENT & HISTORY OF BELGIUM

ABOVE: *The headquarters of the European Union in Brussels.*

EUROPEAN COUNTRIES TODAY: BELGIUM

Today, one of the most pressing political issues facing Belgium is that many people from Dutch-speaking Flanders want the nation's various regions to gain more political power than they have now. Meanwhile the French-speaking Walloons prefer to keep things the way they are, with a strong central government. The debate is ongoing.

Aside from internal politics, Belgium has seen a rise in terrorism. The most recent attack was on Brussels's Zaventem airport and Maalbeek metro station in March 2016. Thirty-five people were killed and 300 injured. As a result, Belgium is on maximum security alert. There is a concern that growth in Islamic extremism amongst immigrant communities in Brussels is fueling these attacks. Despite its problems, Brussels remains the headquarters of NATO and the EU.

Text-Dependent Questions

1. Which part of Africa did Leopold II colonize?

2. Why was Belgium declared a neutral country before World War II?

3. Who is Belgium's current king?

Research Project

Using your research, describe what it was like living in Belgium during World War II under German occupation.

41

THE GOVERNMENT & HISTORY OF BELGIUM

The Formation of the European Union (EU)

The EU is a confederation of European nations that continues to grow. As of 2017, there are twenty-eight official members. Several other candidates are also waiting for approval. All countries that enter the EU agree to follow common laws about foreign security policies. They also agree to cooperate on legal matters that go on within the EU. The European Council meets to discuss all international matters and make decisions about them. Each country's own concerns and interests are important, though. And apart from legal and financial issues, the EU tries to uphold values such as peace, human dignity, freedom, and equality.

All member countries remain autonomous. This means that they generally keep their own laws and regulations. The idea for a union among European nations was first mentioned after World War II. The war had devastated much of Europe, both physically and financially. In 1950, the French foreign minister suggested that France and West Germany combine their coal and steel industries under one authority. Both countries would have control over the

ABOVE: *The entrance to the European Union Parliament Building in Brussels.*

EUROPEAN COUNTRIES TODAY: BELGIUM

MEMBER COUNTRIES

Austria	Greece	Romania
Belgium	Hungary	Slovakia
Bulgaria	Ireland	Slovenia
Croatia	Italy	Spain
Cyprus	Latvia	Sweden
Czech Republic	Lithuania	United Kingdom
Denmark	Luxembourg	*(Brexit: For the time*
Estonia	Malta	*being, the United*
Finland	Netherlands	*Kingdom remains a full*
France	Poland	*member of the EU.)*
Germany	Portugal	

industries. This would help them become more financially stable. It would also make war between the countries much more difficult. The idea was interesting to other European countries as well. In 1951, France, West Germany, Belgium, Luxembourg, the Netherlands, and Italy signed the Treaty of Paris, creating the European Coal and Steel Community. These six countries would become the core of the EU.

In 1957, these same countries signed the Treaties of Rome, creating the European Economic Community. In 1965, the Merger Treaty formed the European Community. Finally, in 1992, the Maastricht Treaty was signed. This treaty defined the European Union. It gave a framework for expanding the EU's political role, particularly in the area of foreign and security policy. It would also replace national currencies with the euro. The next year, the treaty went into effect. At that time, the member countries included the original six plus another six who had joined during the 1970s and '80s.

In the following years, the EU would take more steps to form a single market for its members. This would make joining the union even more advantageous. In addition to enlargement, the EU is steadily becoming more integrated through its own policies for closer cooperation between member states.

Words to Understand

currency: Coin and banknotes in circulation as a medium of exchange.

intergovernmental: Existing or occurring between two or more governments or levels of government.

multinational: Relating to more than two nationalities.

BELOW: Despite being a densely populated nation, Belgium has sparsely inhabited areas of tranquil countryside.

Chapter Three
THE BELGIAN ECONOMY

By keeping its doors open to people, goods, and services from all over the globe, Belgium has made its citizens among the richest in the world. This relatively small country has few natural resources, limited land, and a population of just over ten million, yet by focusing on its strengths—skills in metalworking, a strong base in heavy industry, an extensive transportation network, and easy access to international trade routes—Belgium has become an important financial center in Europe.

ABOVE: *A shop in Bruges selling beer and other products. Belgium has an important brewing industry.*

THE BELGIAN ECONOMY

Industry

By making good use of its skills in metalworking and heavy industry, Belgium has created an industrial base that accounts for 27 percent of the country's gross domestic product (GDP). Most of Belgium's industrial plants are located in the Flanders region, in the corridor between Antwerp and Brussels. Industries such as steel, chemicals, shipbuilding, automobiles, glass, paper, food processing, and heavy machinery employ one-fifth of the Belgian workforce. Belgium's crude petroleum, most of which is imported, is processed in refineries located in Antwerp. Some of the biggest, most brilliant, and most expensive diamonds in the world are cut and sold in Antwerp. Belgium is also one of the world's leading processors of cobalt, radium, copper, zinc, and lead, all of which are imported in their raw form.

ABOVE: Over 80 percent of the world's diamonds pass through Antwerp.

Educational Video

Antwerp and Diamonds— A brilliant story. A look at the fascinating world of Antwerp's diamond industry.

EUROPEAN COUNTRIES TODAY: BELGIUM

ABOVE: *Cooling towers of the nuclear power plant in Doel near Antwerp. Nuclear power produces an important proportion of Belgium's electricity.*

THE BELGIAN ECONOMY

Foreign investment in Belgium brought with it a boom in the country's engineering sector in the late twentieth century. The country has assembly plants for American, Swedish, German, and French automobiles. Most of those cars are imported to the European market. In addition, the car plants in Brussels and Ghent are playing major roles in the electrification of major European brands such as Audi and Volvo, which will be available in 2018 and 2019.

Belgium is also home to large **multinational** corporations manufacturing heavy electrical motors, machine tools, specialized plastics, chemicals, and pharmaceuticals.

ABOVE: Circuit de Spa-Francorchamps motor-racing circuit is the center of Belgium's motor racing industry. It is the venue of the Formula One Belgian Grand Prix, the 24 Hours of Spa, Endurance Cup, and other important races.

EUROPEAN COUNTRIES TODAY: BELGIUM

ABOVE: *Brussels International Airport is on the edge of the city and serves both premium and budget airlines.*

Services

Throughout history, Belgium has offered the world a convenient place to conduct business. Located at the crossroads of Europe, Belgium is a takeoff point for trade and traffic between Europe and the Americas. Large service industries from all over the world have taken advantage of Belgium's location.

Banking, information technology, insurance, recruitment, travel, and tourism account for 71 percent of the Belgian economy and employ two-thirds of the Belgian workforce. Thousands of Belgians are also employed by the many EU, NATO, and other intergovernmental offices based in Brussels.

THE BELGIAN ECONOMY

Belgium's small fishing industry is based in the coastal towns of Zeebrugge and Ostend along the North Sea. All products of the fishing industry are used within the country itself.

The planted forests of the Ardennes and the Kempenland support Belgium's relatively small forest products industry. Mechanization has helped growth in the forest industry, allowing Belgium to reduce its reliance on imported timber.

Natural Resources

Coal and Metallic Ores: Belgium's most important mineral resources, coal and metallic ores, have been depleted. The coal needs of the steel industry, thermal power plants, and for domestic heating are met through imports. Belgium also imports large quantities of iron ore and zinc, since the refining of metallic ores is an important component of Belgium's economy.

Chalk, Limestone, Sand, Clay, and Marble: The mining of chalk and limestone supports a significant cement industry in Wallonia. Sand is mined in the Kempenland for use in glass manufacturing. In Borinage, clay is mined for pottery products and bricks. Stone, mostly marble, is also quarried.

Water: Belgium has plenty of water, but most of it is concentrated in the southern part of the country in the form of streams and groundwater. However, most of Belgium's population lives in the north. To meet the country's needs, Belgium has elaborate water-transfer systems involving canals, storage basins, and pipelines. Today, the key problem facing Belgium is water pollution caused largely by industries located along Belgium's main rivers.

Economic Crisis

In 2008, Belgium (along with most of the rest of the world) faced a major financial crisis. Two of the country's largest banks, Fortis and Dexia, were in trouble. The value of their stocks, as well as the stocks of most other Belgian companies, plunged. The government tried to control the situation by bailing out banks and guaranteeing bank deposits. Eventually, Fortis was split into two

EUROPEAN COUNTRIES TODAY: BELGIUM

parts: the government took over the Dutch part, while the Belgian part was sold to the French bank BNP Paribas. Besides the bailouts of both Fortis and Dexia, the government also guaranteed all bank savings up to €20,000.

The subdued economic growth over the past decade is projected to improve in 2017 and 2018. Private investment is the main driver of growth, and a pick-up in international trade will help support exports. Neighboring countries have a strong political and economic impact on Belgium. However, the terrorist attacks in March 2016 have cost the nation billions in additional security measures and lost business and tax revenue. Tourism has been particularly affected.

An ageing population means that health-care costs are rising at the same time, which puts additional stress on the country's economy.

Text-Dependent Questions

1. When did Belgium adopt the euro?

2. What are Belgium's two main rivers?

3. Where is Belgium's forestry industry located?

Research Project

Belgium's economy is inextricably tied to that of Europe. Who are the country's major trading partners and what are its most important exports and imports?

Words to Understand

chauvinism: Undue attachment to a place or group that one belongs to.

ethnic: Relating to a specified ethnic group.

vulgar: Ostentatious or excessive.

BELOW: Brussels, the capital of Belgium, has two official languages, so all road signs and government documents are printed in French and Dutch.

Chapter Four
CITIZENS OF BELGIUM: PEOPLE, CUSTOMS & CULTURE

What Belgium lacks in size, it makes up for in density. Although the country has a population of only a little over ten million, Belgium has one of the highest population densities in Europe. On an average, nearly 336 Belgians are crammed into every square kilometer. As only 4 percent of the population lives in rural areas, population density varies from a scant 140 persons per square mile on the Ardennes plateau to 15,300 per square mile in the Brussels-Capital Region.

The Two Faces of Belgium

Belgians have a quirky sense of humor and an appetite for life. Yet the bonhomie of everyday Belgian life conceals a country that is fractured into two linguistic communities. The Dutch-speaking Flemings live in Flanders in the north, and the French-speaking Walloons live in Wallonia in the south. Caught between this deep language divide is the officially bilingual capital city of Brussels.

The bitter **ethnic** tensions between these two communities have ensured that today Belgium is less a country and more an administrative entity: the French- and Flemish-speaking regions survive as virtually two separate federal states.

The Flemings are the dominant community in Belgium. They make up nearly 60 percent of the region's population and hold most of the nation's wealth. The Flemings are industrious, honest, and cultured people who are not showy or **vulgar**.

The Walloons make up just over 30 percent of the Belgian population. Although the Walloons once controlled Belgium's coal mines and industries, their economic prosperity declined with the closure of the mines. Proud of their past, and somewhat defensive of their present, Walloons are liberal minded, sociable, and good-natured.

CITIZENS OF BELGIUM: PEOPLE, CUSTOMS & CULTURE

ABOVE: *Our Blessed Lady of the Sablon Church has a history that dates back to the thirteenth century. It is located in the Sablon district in the historic center of Brussels. It is characterized by its late Brabantine Gothic exterior.*

Belgium also has a tiny German-speaking community living in the areas bordering Germany in the east. In Wallonia, three additional regional languages are officially recognized: Champenois, Gaumais, and Picard.

Religion: Looking to Rome

Religion was one of the reasons that Catholic Belgium broke away from the Protestant north of the United Kingdom of the Netherlands in 1830. Today, more than 80 percent of Belgians are Roman Catholic. Islam, Protestantism, and Judaism are other religions widely practiced in Belgium. Many brotherhoods and secret societies were also established in Belgium in the mid-twentieth century.

EUROPEAN COUNTRIES TODAY: BELGIUM

Education: A Very Intensive System

Over 99 percent of the adult population in Belgium can read and write. Education is obligatory from age six to eighteen, but most Belgian young adults continue studying until they are twenty-three years old. This makes Belgium's education system the second-most intensive in Europe (the United Kingdom's is even more demanding). Belgium has an educational system composed of two parts: state secular schools and private denominational (mostly Roman Catholic) schools. Both kinds of school are given similar financial assistance by the government. Belgium has several universities as well as other specialized institutions of higher education.

ABOVE: *As Belgium is divided into distinct federal regions, there are separate education systems for each of the communities.*

CITIZENS OF BELGIUM: PEOPLE, CUSTOMS & CULTURE

Food and Drink

To put it mildly, Belgians' appetite for life extends across the language divide. Chocolate is the country's most-recognized export. Traditional Belgian chocolates, some of which are known as pralines, are filled with cream, liqueurs, nuts, or ganache, and are considered by many the best in the world.

As for daily fare, Belgium's two linguistic regions are reflected in the country's cuisine. Fish and crustaceans are prominent in Flemish cuisine, reflecting the Dutch influence on the Flemish. Walloon cuisine tends to be more substantial, more spicy, and to have more calories than either Flemish or modern French cuisine.

Beer can rightly be called the Belgian national drink, even though Belgians rank fifth as consumers of beer in Europe. Until 1900, every village had its own brewery, with more than three thousand in Wallonia alone. Today, there are 180 breweries in Belgium. Together, they brew more than four hundred varieties of beer.

ABOVE: Mussels and fries is a popular main dish originating in Belgium.

EUROPEAN COUNTRIES TODAY: BELGIUM

Belgian Waffles
Belgians eat these as a dessert rather than a breakfast food.

Makes 8 servings

Ingredients
2¼ teaspoons active dry yeast
¼ cup plus 2 ¾ cups warm milk, divided
3 eggs, divided
¾ cup butter, melted
½ cup granulated sugar
¾ teaspoon salt
1½ teaspoon vanilla extract
4 cups all-purpose flour

Directions
In a small bowl, dissolve the yeast in ¼ cup warm milk. Beat the egg whites just until stiff peaks form. In a large bowl, mix together the egg yolks, ¼ cup of the remaining milk, the melted butter, and the sugar. Add the yeast mixture, salt, vanilla, and then alternate between the flour and remaining milk. Gently fold the egg whites into the waffle batter. Cover the batter without touching it, and then set it in a warm place to rise until it doubles in volume, about 1 hour. Cook in a waffle iron according to manufacturer's instructions.

Gourmet Belgian Hot Chocolate

Ingredients
4 cups milk
1 vanilla bean, split lengthwise
7 ounces bittersweet chocolate, chopped into small pieces

Directions
Heat the milk and the vanilla bean in a saucepan over a medium heat. When bubbles appear around the edges, reduce the flame and add the chocolate. Whisk until the chocolate has completely melted, then remove from heat. Carefully remove the vanilla bean. If the chocolate is too thick, thin with additional milk. Whisk vigorously just before serving to create a foamy head. Add sugar if required.

CITIZENS OF BELGIUM: PEOPLE, CUSTOMS & CULTURE

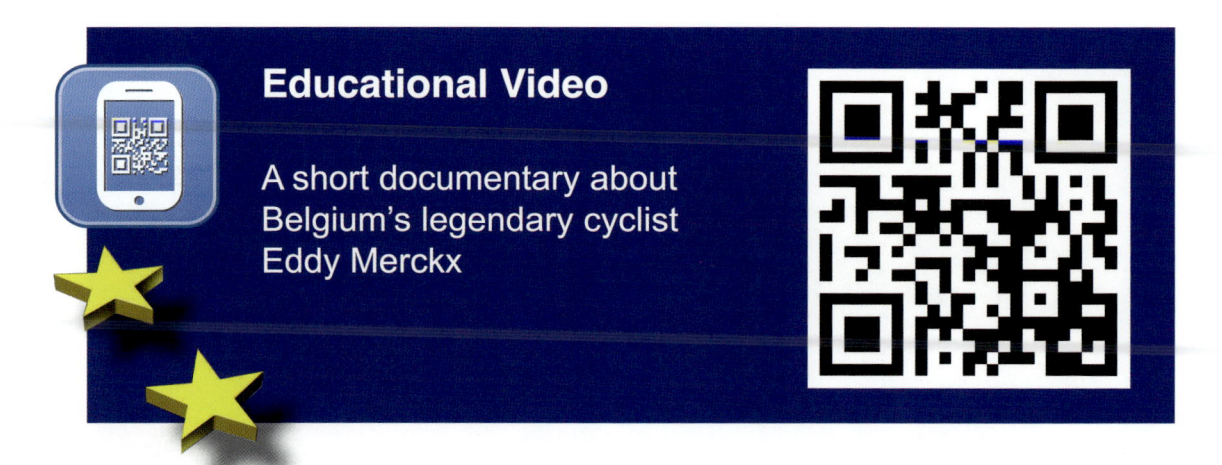

Educational Video

A short documentary about Belgium's legendary cyclist Eddy Merckx

Sports

Sports often makes Belgians put their linguistic **chauvinism** aside and join together. A national passion for cycling has produced Belgium's greatest sportsman to date. Racing cyclist Eddy Merckx won the Tour de France five times, as well as more than 140 other major titles. Auto racing driver Jacky Ickx won eight Formula One Grand Prix races.

Soccer is also a popular sport. Although Belgium has never won any major international competitions, such as the World Cup or European Championships, it stands a respectable tenth in the FIFA rankings for world soccer.

Belgium has always been known for producing top-class tennis players. Justine Henin, Kim Clijsters, David Goffin, Xavier Malise, Kirsten Flipkens, Yanina Wickmayer, and Filip Dewulf have all ranked highly in recent years.

Festivals: Celebrations Galore

Belgians love to celebrate. Along with the major religious festivals, Belgians celebrate their country's independence on National Day, July 21. Some of Belgium's biggest festivals revolve around Christian events, even though Christmas itself is a low-key affair.

Four weeks before Lent, the Walloon town of Binche hosts a carnival, featuring gilles, or clown-like figures. In Flanders, the most important religious festival is the Procession of the Holy Blood in Bruges. The procession

EUROPEAN COUNTRIES TODAY: BELGIUM

centers on a precious religious relic, a crystal vial supposedly containing the blood of Christ.

Across Belgium, small towns and large cities boast some rather unorthodox celebrations, giving further proof that Belgians will create reasons to celebrate if none can be found. Striking examples are the Cat's Festival in Ypres, the Windmill Festival in Lembeke, the Witches' Procession in Nieuwpoort, and the Peasants' Festival in Turnhout.

ABOVE: *The Annual Procession of the Holy Blood on Ascension Day, Bruges. Locals perform an historical reenactment and dramatizations of Biblical events.*

CITIZENS OF BELGIUM: PEOPLE, CUSTOMS & CULTURE

Peter Paul Rubens (1577–1640)

Peter Paul Rubens was a Flemish artist. He was born in the town of Siegen, Westphalia (now Germany). At the age of ten, the family moved to Antwerp, where Rubens was trained to be an artist. He served several apprenticeships and in 1598 joined the Antwerp guild for painters. He is considered the most important artist of Flemish baroque tradition. His unique and immensely popular baroque style emphasized movement, color, and sensuality. Rubens specialized in making altarpieces, portraits, landscapes, and history paintings of mythological and allegorical subjects. Rubens ran a large studio in Antwerp that produced paintings popular with nobility and art collectors throughout Europe. Rubens's work was admired by many of his contemporaries including Rembrandt and at his death on May 30, 1640, was one of the most celebrated artists in Europe.

Art and Architecture

Flemish art flowered during the Renaissance of the fifteenth century. The leading painter of the time, Jan van Eyck, perfected the technique of oil painting and is considered by many art historians to be the first successful painter working in oils. Within the next hundred years, a distinct Flemish style developed, led by Pieter Brueghel the Elder and his two sons, Pieter Brueghel the Younger and Jan Brueghel the Elder. Pieter Brueghel was famous for placing classical or religious events in the contemporary setting of a Flemish village.

EUROPEAN COUNTRIES TODAY: BELGIUM

The Arnolfini Marriage. By Jan van Eyck. Oil on board 1434.

65

CITIZENS OF BELGIUM: PEOPLE, CUSTOMS & CULTURE

Rubens and Isabella Brandt, the Honeysuckle Bower by Peter Paul Rubens. Oil on Canvas 1609.

Belgium's next great artist was Peter Paul Reubens (1577–1640), one of Europe's greatest artists of the baroque period. Among his many paintings is the ceiling of the Banqueting House in London's Whitehall. He was also among the artists who produced designs for tapestries. From the fifteenth to the eighteenth century, Flanders led the world in the production of tapestries.

In the twentieth century, the surrealist movement produced an explosion of striking and subversive images that reflected the avant-garde's desire to scandalize and unsettle. René Magritte and Paul Delvaux were among the leading artists of surrealism.

The architecture of Belgium's cities reflects the country's history as the melting pot of Europe. Traces of Austrian, Spanish, French, and Dutch influences can be seen throughout the country. Perhaps the greatest Belgian architect is Victor Horta, whose Hotel Tassel is the "earliest monument of art nouveau."

ABOVE: Hotel Tassel in Brussels. By architect, Victor Horta.

Music

Dutch and French traditions strongly influenced Belgian folk music, with wind and percussion instruments giving energetic company to the accordion. Belgium has also nurtured the talents of some world-class violinists,

CITIZENS OF BELGIUM: PEOPLE, CUSTOMS & CULTURE

including Arthur Grumiaux, Eugène Ysaÿe, Henri Vieuxtemps, and Charles Auguste de Bériot.

Jazz music has Belgium to thank for its most popular instrument. Belgian Adolphe Sax invented the saxophone in 1845. Using the stage name Johnny Hallyday, Belgian Jean-Philippe Smets became France's equivalent to Elvis Presley.

Literature

Belgium has produced one of the most popular writers of the twentieth century. Georges Simenon, creator of Inspector Maigret, published over three hundred novels, mainly on crime subjects. To date, more than 500 million copies of his books have been sold, making Simenon one of the most widely read authors in the world. His books have been translated into many languages and have been adapted for film and television.

ABOVE: *Henri Vieuxtemps. Lithograph by Josef Kriehuber, 1842.*

One of the most famous Belgian literary figures is not an author at all. Inspector Hercule Poirot appeared in thirty-three novels and sixty-five short stories by British author Agatha Christie. Many of the tales were adapted for film and television. When other characters asked the rotund detective if he were French, he took much delight in telling them he was Belgian. After the much-beloved character died in the book Curtain (1975), Hercule Poirot became the only fictional character honored with an obituary on the front page of the New York Times.

EUROPEAN COUNTRIES TODAY: BELGIUM

Georges Remi (who took the pen name Hergé) drew *The Adventures of Tintin.* Beginning as a newspaper cartoon, these stories have now sold over 140 million copies in book form. They have been translated into all the major languages of the world.

Joining Remi is a plethora of noted Belgian cartoonists including André Franquin, Pierre Culliford, and Jean Roba. Brussels is home to the Belgian Comic Strip Center.

ABOVE: *The Belgian Comic Strip Center, Brussels.*

Text-Dependent Questions

1. What are the two official languages of Brussels?

2. Name three important sports in Belgium.

3. What painting technique did Jan van Eyck perfect?

Research Project

Study the Arnolfini Marriage painting on page 65 and, using Internet resources, write about the hidden symbolism in the painting.

Words to Understand

agglomeration: A large and densely populated city and its surrounding suburbs.

flea market: A market for secondhand items and antiques.

tributary: A stream feeding a larger stream, river, or lake.

BELOW: Guildhalls at the Grand Place in Brussels.

Chapter Five
THE FAMOUS CITIES OF BELGIUM

Belgium is the third-most urbanized country in the world, ranking only behind Singapore and Kuwait. Over 97 percent of its population live in cities. The Belgian cities are ranked among the most splendid in Europe. In Flanders, picturesque towns, dazzling port cities, and living museums such as Ghent, Antwerp, and Bruges dot the network of rivers and canals. In Wallonia, the cities of Liège, Namur, and Tournai are set amid the forests of the Ardennes. In the center of the country is Brussels, the capital.

Brussels

Founded over one thousand years ago on the banks of the Senne, a **tributary** of the river Scheldt, Brussels is often described as the capital of Europe. It is home to the EU, NATO, and other international organizations, giving the city a cosmopolitan feel.

Brussels is the third-richest region in Europe. Its economy is primarily based on services and manufacturing. With office of several national and multinational corporations, the city is an important transportation and communications hub. It is a manufacturing point for

ABOVE: Brussels's town hall is situated in a beautiful square called the Grand Place.

71

THE FAMOUS CITIES OF BELGIUM

Educational Video

Things to do in Brussels. Visit the attractions that Brussels is most famous for and move on to explore lesser-known areas.

ABOVE: *The Kunstberg or Mont des Arts are formal gardens on top of a hill. Other major tourist attractions and museums are located within easy walking distance from the gardens.*

EUROPEAN COUNTRIES TODAY: BELGIUM

ABOVE: Brussels old town. There are many ancient winding streets off the Grand Place. They are full of restaurants and shops that are popular with tourists and locals alike.

steel, chemicals, machinery, textiles, electrical equipment, and pharmaceuticals. Brussels is also a printing and publishing center. Telecommunications, precision engineering, and other high-technology industries are expanding.

Explosive growth has engulfed Brussels and the surrounding countryside. The expansion has also swallowed up the river on which it is situated. Today, the Brussels-Capital Region, also called Greater Brussels, is the country's largest urban **agglomeration**. The region consists of nineteen administratively independent communities that form a regional metropolis.

THE FAMOUS CITIES OF BELGIUM

Antwerp

Hugging the eastern bank of the Scheldt, Antwerp is Belgium's second-largest city (after Brussels) and its busiest port. Antwerp is renowned as one of the world's main centers for diamond dealing, cutting, and polishing. The city is an industrial nucleus as well as a center for art.

Until 1859, Antwerp was surrounded by its sixteenth-century fortified walls, within which lies the old city. The area contains the Cathedral of Our Lady, one of the country's finest examples of Gothic architecture. By the latter half of the

ABOVE: *The Grote Markt (Great Market Square) of Antwerp is situated in the heart of the old city quarter. The square is famous for its many beautiful guildhalls.*

EUROPEAN COUNTRIES TODAY: BELGIUM

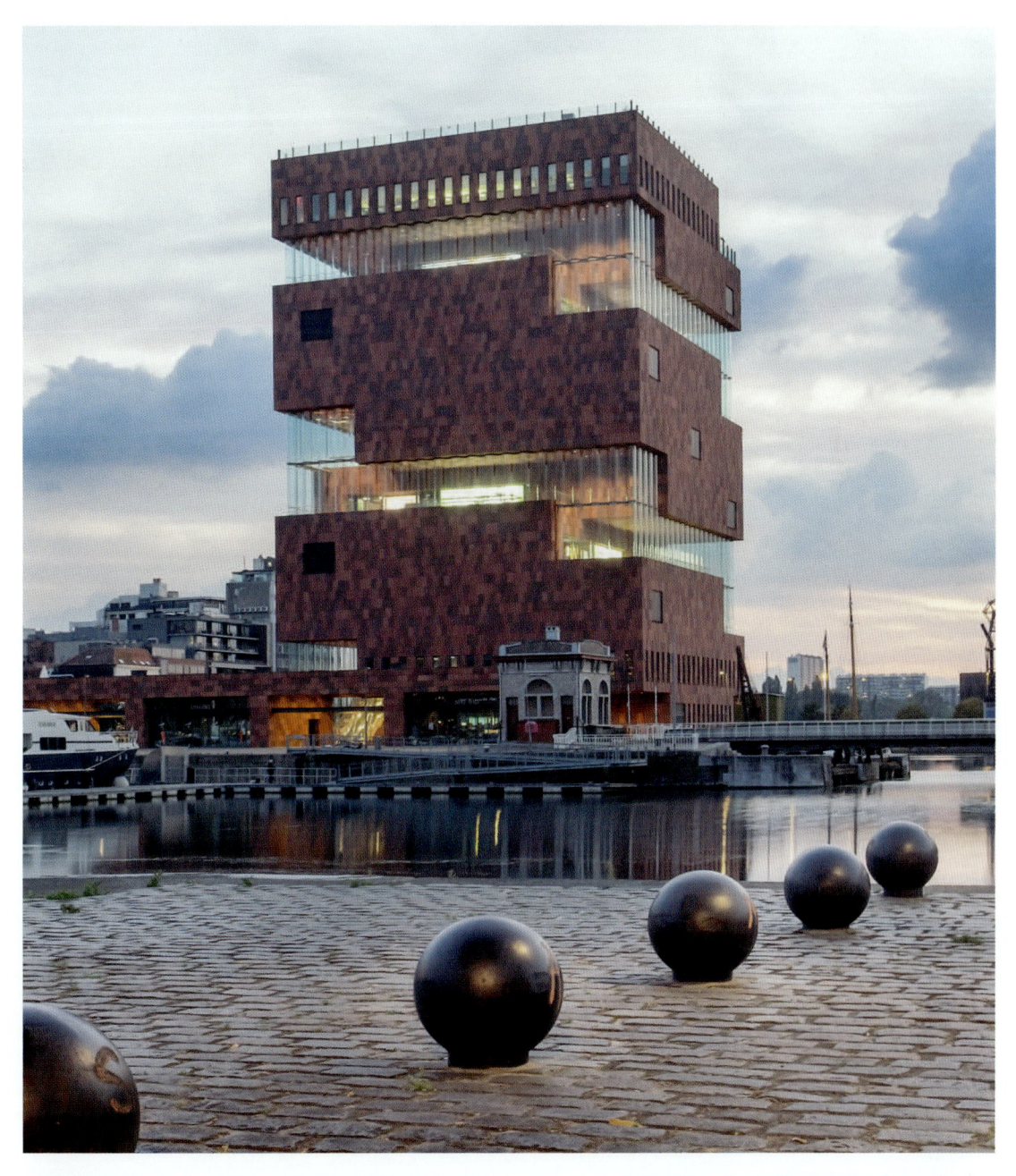

ABOVE: *The Museum aan de Stroom is a located along the river Scheldt in the Eilandje district of Antwerp, Belgium. It opened in May 2011 and is the largest museum in Antwerp.*

THE FAMOUS CITIES OF BELGIUM

ABOVE: The Collegiate Church of St. Bartholomew in Liège. Founded outside the city walls and dating back to the twelfth century, it was built in coal sandstone.

nineteenth century, these walls were transformed into broad avenues as a larger semicircle of fortifications was built.

The largest part of Antwerp, however, is is taken up by the essentially nonresidential northern seaport and industrial areas. Long-established chemical plants, shipbuilders, and automobile factories crowd together, joined by newer factories that produce photographic and electronic equipment.

Antwerp's cultural past has been preserved. The homes and workshops of sixteenth-century printer Christophe Plantin and seventeenth-century painter Peter Paul Rubens have been made into museums.

Liège

Located at the junction of the Meuse and the Ourthe rivers in eastern Belgium, Liège is a university city. Situated near the German border, it is also the steel

EUROPEAN COUNTRIES TODAY: BELGIUM

ABOVE: *Montagne de Bueren is a 374-step staircase in Liège. The staircase is named after Vincent de Bueren, who defended Liège against an attack by the Duke of Burgundy in the fifteenth century. It was built in 1881 to honor the 600 soldiers who died in the battle.*

THE FAMOUS CITIES OF BELGIUM

center of Belgium. Liège is the third-largest inland port in Europe, after Duisburg and Paris.

During the Middle Ages, Liège was a city of craftsmen, particularly goldsmiths, silversmiths, and arms manufacturers. Although it was the first city in Europe to mine coal, as new fuels became more popular, coal mining eventually ground to a halt. Other industries, such as metalworking plants, stone quarries and gravel, and cement factories persist.

Liège also has one of the largest pedestrian areas in Europe, consisting of more than five thousand shops. Shoppers can also visit La Batte, one of the largest **flea markets** in the country, where visitors can browse for all manner of treasures, big and small.

ABOVE: *The city of Liège beside the river Meuse.*

EUROPEAN COUNTRIES TODAY: BELGIUM

ABOVE: The Guildhalls at Graslei, which is a quay in the historic city center of Ghent, located on the right bank of the Leie River.

Ghent

Built over canalized waterways of the Leie and Scheldt rivers, Ghent is a vibrant city of industry and maritime trade. It is also the second-largest port of Belgium. Ghent has been the focal point of Flemish nationality for centuries. On December 24, 1814, the Treaty of Ghent was signed here, which marked the end of the War of 1812 between the United States and Britain.

For a long time, Ghent was the center of the Belgian textile industry. Today, the city's economy revolves around the oil refining, chemical, steel, and automotive industries. Publishing and banking are major activities. Ghent is

THE FAMOUS CITIES OF BELGIUM

also a center of horticulture and market gardening. Its great flower show, Les Floralies, is held every five years.

Tourism is also a significant contributor to the city's prosperity. Ghent has retained more traces of its past than any other Belgian city. The feudal castle of the counts of Flanders is one of the most imposing castles to have survived in Europe. Ghent is home to the famous Ghent Altarpiece, *The Adoration of the Mystic Lamb*, by the artist Jan van Eyck.

ABOVE: *The cafés and bars in Ghent are renowned for their fine beer, food, and atmosphere.*

EUROPEAN COUNTRIES TODAY: BELGIUM

ABOVE: Dating back to 942 CE, St. Bavo's Cathedral, Ghent. This beautiful Gothic building is the seat of the diocese of Ghent.

THE FAMOUS CITIES OF BELGIUM

Bruges

The capital of the province of West Flanders, Bruges is often called the "Venice of the North" because of its many canals. The city is the home of one of Europe's first stock exchanges. It is also the hometown of the renowned Flemish painter Jan van Eyck.

Like Ghent, Bruges owes its prosperous past to the cloth trade. However, when the Zwijn estuary, which gave Bruges access to the sea, silted up in the fifteenth century, the city began to decline as a trade center. Bruges did not

ABOVE: *Bruges suffered little damage during World War II and today is a UNESCO World Heritage Site.*

EUROPEAN COUNTRIES TODAY: BELGIUM

ABOVE: *The Quay of the Rosary (Rozenhoedkaai) is one of the most photographed sites in Bruges.*

THE FAMOUS CITIES OF BELGIUM

regain its status as an ocean port until the early twentieth-century construction of a canal connecting it with Zeebrugge on the North Sea coast.

Today, as a rail and canal junction, Bruges is an important market for grain, cattle, horses, engineering, ship repairing, electrical goods, glassmaking, textiles, and lace. However, Bruges's largest industry is tourism. The city plays host to the most important festival in Flanders, the annual Holy Blood Procession.

ABOVE: *Jambes Bridge spans the river Meuse at Namur in the French speaking Wallonia region of Belgium.*

EUROPEAN COUNTRIES TODAY: BELGIUM

Namur

Nestled in the foothills of the Ardennes, Namur is a transportation hub for southern Belgium. The city is dominated by its medieval citadel, which sits atop a rocky outcrop between the Meuse and Sambre rivers.

Because of its strategic position at the head of routes into France, Namur has been the scene of many battles and sieges. Not until the eighteenth century, under the rule of the Dutch, were many of Namur's broad boulevards laid out. The Dutch were also responsible for restoring the citadel, which is the dominant feature of Namur's skyline.

A rail junction and center of art, Namur is also an industrial town. Glass, paper, leather goods, steel products, and cement are manufactured here. Tourism is also a major industry. Namur's castles, citadels, and cathedrals attract thousands of tourists each year.

Text-Dependent Questions

1. What is the capital city of Belgium?

2. Who was Christophe Plantin?

3. Why is Bruges often called the "Venice of the North"?

Research Project

Antwerp is the largest diamond trading center in the world. Document the history of the diamond industry in Antwerp and explain why the city is so important for the Belgian economy.

Words to Understand

abdication: The act of renouncing a responsibility.

autonomous: Self-governing and independent.

coalition: A combination or alliance between persons, countries, or factions.

BELOW: *The financial district of Brussels today.*

Chapter Six
A BRIGHT FUTURE FOR BELGIUM

Belgium was occupied by the Germans during two World Wars, and suffered severe devastation. Baudouin became king in 1951, after the **abdication** of Leopold III.

Flemish is spoken mainly in Flanders in the north, and French and Walloon, a French dialect, in Wallonia in the south. Rivalry between the two factions led to disputes over language and calls for regional self-government in the 1970s. In 1993 a federal system of government was adopted with three parliaments, Flanders, Wallonia, and Brussels, which afforded recognition and autonomy to the regions at last. That year, King Baudouin died and was succeeded by his brother, Albert II. The reign of Albert II lasted until his abdication for health reasons in 2013. The new king of the Belgians was his son Philippe, who continues as head of state. The current prime minister is Charles Michel, who has been in office since 2014.

Belgium made a rapid recovery after World War II and has made good economic progress ever since. It became one of the Benelux countries with the Netherlands and Luxembourg in 1948. This, and the

ABOVE: *EU and Belgian flags.*

A BRIGHT FUTURE FOR BELGIUM

ABOVE: *King Philippe and Queen Mathilde wave to the crowds in Brussels.*

geography of its position, gave it significant influence in Europe, and it became a founder member of the European Community, with Brussels now providing the administrative headquarters of the EU.

Belgium's only significant mineral resource is coal, but it produces textiles, vehicles, and chemicals among other commodities. It must therefore rely on export of its manufactured goods, which makes it economically dependent on the conditions of world markets.

Belgium's economy is well-positioned to grow further in the twenty-first century. With a thriving export-driven economy, it is likely to operate with a trade surplus for the forseeable future. Belgium's infrastructure and links to

EUROPEAN COUNTRIES TODAY: BELGIUM

other European countries secures its position in the world as being a trading hub for goods and services. The introduction of the single currency in Europe has also helped the Belgian economy immensely. Domestically, Belgium faces a variety of problems. Continuing tension between the Dutch-and French-speaking populations has led to the division of the nation into semi-**autonomous** regions that compete with one another for economic growth and investment. In addition, the unemployment rate remains stubbornly high, although it has improved recently.

Looking to the future, Belgium is well placed to continue to be a modern, adaptable, and successful country. As a united Europe stands to become the most powerful **coalition** of all the countries in the world, Belgium stands at its center. It is a shining example of how individual countries can come together to work for a brighter future.

Text Dependent Questions

1. Why is Belgium's geographical position important?

2. What countries make up Benelux?

3. Where is the administrative center of the EU?

Research Project

Write a well-researched paper on the history of Belgium's most important industries, which have enabled it to develop into the modern country it is today.

INDEX

Infant mortality rate, 9
Intergovernmental agencies, 47
Islam, 9, 58
Islamic extremism, 41
Italy, 36, 43

J
Jambes Bridge, 84
Judaism, 58

K
Kempenland, 54
Kempen Plains, 13
Kingdom of Belgium, origin, 25
King Leopold I (Dawe), 34
Knokke, 52
Kunstberg (Mont des Arts), 72
Kuwait, 71

Lace, 32
Languages, 9
    bi-lingualism, 57
    divisions, 57
Leie River, 52, 79
Lembeke, 63
Lent, 62
Leopold
    I, 34
    II, 34, 35
    III, 38
    of Saxe-Coburg, 25
Leopold II, 35
Les Floralies, 80
Liège, 16, 19, 52, 53, 71, 76–78
Life expectancy, 9
Limburg, 19
Literacy rate, 8, 59
Literature, 68–69
Location, 7, 51
Luxembourg (Grand Duchy of), 7, 11, 36, 43, 87
Luxembourg (province), 19

M
Maalbeek metro station, 41
Maastricht Treaty, 43
Magritte, René, 67
Maigret, Inspector, 68
Malise, Xavier, 62
Map, 6
Maria Theresa, Queen, 32, 33
Maria Theresa (Meytens), 33
Marie of Burgundy, 30, 32
Marie of Burgundy (Pacher), 30
Maximilian I, 31, 32
Maximilian I, Holy Roman Emperor (Dürer), 31
Mediterranean, 27
Menin Gate, 37
Merckx, Eddy, 62
Merger Treaty, 43
Metalworking and heavy industry, 48
Meuse river, 14, 18, 19, 53, 76–78, 84, 85
Meytens, Martin van, 33
Michel, Charles, 87
Migration rate, 9
Montagne de Bueren, 77
Motor racing, 50
Multinational corporations, 50
Museum aan de Stroom, 75
Music, 67–68
    folk, 67
    jazz, 68
Mussels and fries, 60

N
Name origin, 25
Namur, 15, 16, 18, 19, 71, 84, 85
National
    Bank, 52
    Day, 62
Natural resources, 54

Netherlands, 7, 11, 13, 25, 34, 36, 43, 47, 87
Nieuwpoort, 63
North Atlantic Treaty Organization (NATO), 18, 41, 51, 71
North Sea, 7, 8, 27, 53, 54, 84
Nuclear power, 49, 53

O
Occupation, war, 87
Ostend, 52, 53, 54
Our Blessed Lady of the Sablon Church, 58
Ourthe river, 76–78

P
Pacher, Michael, 30
Parliaments, 87
Peasants' Festival, 63
People, 9
Philip
    Duke of Burgundy, 30, 32
    II of Spain, 32
Philip, Duke of Burgundy (Weyden), 30
Philippe, 38, 87
Picard, 58
Plantin, Christopher, 76
Plants, 21–22
Poirot, Hercule, 68
Polder Zone, 12
Poppy, 14
Population, 9, 57
    age, 9
    growth rate, 9
Prime minister, 87
Procession of the Holy Blood, 62–63, 84
Protestantism, 9, 32, 58
Provinces, 8, 19

INDEX

Q
Quay of the Rosary (Rozenhoedkaai), 83

R
Railroads, 53
Religion, 9, 34, 58
Remi, Georges, 69
Resistance, 36
Revolt of the Netherlands, 32
Rivers, 19
Road signs, 56
Roadways, 53
Roba, Jean, 69
Roche-en-Ardenne, La, 26
Rochefort, 15
Roman Catholicism, 9, 32, 58
Roman Empire, 27
Royal Castle of Laeken, 39
Rubber, 35
Rubens, Peter Paul, 64, 66, 67, 76
Rubens and Isabella Brandt, the Honeysuckle Bower (Rubens), 66

S
Sambre river, 85
Savings Bank of the General Savings and Pensions Fund, 52
Sax, Adolphe, 68
Saxophone, 68
Scheldt river, 12, 17, 19, 53, 71, 73, 74, 75, 79
Semois River, 10, 22
Senne, 17, 71, 73
Services industry, 51
Signal de Botrange, 7, 14
Simenon, George, 68
Singapore, 71
Smets, Jean-Philippe, 68
Soccer, 62
Société Générale de Belgique, 52
Spanish rule, 32
Sports, 62
St. Bavo's Cathedral, 81
Steel industry, 16
Stocks, 54
Surrealist movement, 67
Switzerland, 25

T
Tapestries, 67
Tennis, 62
Terrain, 7
Terrorism, 41
Textile industry, 30, 79, 82
Topographical zones, 12
Tour de France, 62
Tourism, 52, 55, 80, 84
Tournai, 16, 19, 71
Transportation, 16, 53, 85
Treaties of Rome, 43
Treaty
   of Ghent, 79
   of Paris, 43
   of Rome, 38
Turnhout, 63
24 hours of Spa, 50

U
UNESCO World Heritage Site, 82
United Kingdom, 25
   of the Netherlands, 34
United States, 79
   of Belgium, 34
Universities, 59
Urbanization, 71

V
"Venice of the North," 82
Vienna, 32
Vieuxtemps, Henri, 68
Vlassenbroek, 8
Volvo, 50

W
Waffles, 61
Waimes, 16
Wallonia, 11, 14, 16, 17, 53, 57, 71, 84, 87
Walloon, 87
   Brabant, 19
   cuisine, 60
   language, 8
Walloons, 57
Warchenne "quartzite," 16
Water, 54
   pollution, 54
Waterways, 53
West
   Flanders, 19, 82
   Germany, 36, 42, 43
Weyden, Rogier van der, 30
Wickmayer, Yanina, 62
Windmill Festival, 63
Witches' Procession, 63
World War
   I, 14, 35, 87
   II, 14, 35–36, 42, 87

Y
Ypres, 35, 37, 63
Ysaÿe, Eugène, 68

Z
Zaventem airport, 41
Zeebrugge, 54
Zwijn estuary, 82

Picture Credits

All images in this book are in the public domain or have been supplied under license by © Shutterstock.com. The publisher credits the following images as follows:

Page 16: Nancy Beijersbergan, page 17: Capture PB, page 18: Lev Levin, page 19: JJ Fara, page 26: T.W. van Urk, page 28: SavvapantPhoto, page 39: Philip Lange, page 42: Roman Yanushevsky, page 45: Pecold, page 50: Oscar Schuler, page 51: EQRoy, page 52: Anton_Ivanov, page 63: DR Travel Photo and Video, page 75: Santi Rodriguez, page 79, 80: Roman Babin, page 88 Marcus Wissman.

Wikimedia Commons and the following:
page 67: Karl Stas, page 69: TADOR.

To the best knowledge of the publisher, all images not specifically credited are in the public domain. If any image has been inadvertently uncredited, please notify the publisher, so that credit can be given in future printings.

Video Credits

Page 12 Geography Now!: http://x-qr.net/1DwL
page 26 Wonderful Wanderingsl: http://x-qr.net/1EW3
page 48 leadingeye: http://x-qr.net/1FhP
page 62 WalrusRider: http://x-qr.net/1HSG
page 72 Dalia's Ambitions: http://x-qr.net/1GKG

Author

Dominic J. Ainsley is a freelance writer on history, geography, and the arts and the author of many books on travel. His passion for traveling dates from when he visited Europe at the age of ten with his parents. Today, Dominic travels the world for work and pleasure, documenting his experiences and encounters as he goes. He lives in the south of England in the United Kingdom with his wife and two children.